Presented to:

Rosi

Presented by:

Children's Worship

Date:

May 2005

Thanks for Being a

TEACHER

Thanks for Being a Teacher

©2004 ELM HILL BOOKS
ISBN: 1-40418-5313

Manuscript written and compiled by Rebecca Currington in association with Snapdragon Editorial Group, Inc.

Cover and Interior design by JacksonDesignCo, llc

Introduction

Thank You for Being a Teacher has been created for the sole purpose of celebrating the role our teachers have played in our lives. It is intended to serve as a simple and earnest word of thanks for all the information, insight, and inspiration they've provided for us through the years.

As you read, we hope you will be moved to outwardly express your love and respect for the amazing teachers who have graced your life. Honor them for answering the call to teach, setting a worthy example, carrying on with patience, and sharing their insights. And then join with us, as we praise those who do the godly work of grooming us for life.

The Publishers

*T*eaching is a partnership with God.

You are not molding iron nor chiseling marble;

you are working with the Creator of the universe

in shaping human character and determining destiny.

——— ✳ ———

RUTH VAUGHN

Table of Contents

Teaching is not just a job. It is a human service

and it must be thought of as a mission.

———— ✳ ————

DR. RALPH TYLER

A Teacher's Calling

Warn the freeloaders to get a move on.
Gently encourage the stragglers, and reach out for
the exhausted, pulling them to their feet. Be patient
with each other, attentive to individual needs.

---✳---

1 THESSALONIANS 5:14 THE MESSAGE

The whole art of teaching

is only the art of awakening

the natural curiosity of young minds

for the purpose of satisfying it afterward.

ANATOLE FRANCE

No teacher should strive
to make men think as he thinks,
but to lead them to the living Truth,
to the Master himself, of whom alone
they can learn anything.

———— ✳ ————

GEORGE MACDONALD

One good teacher in a lifetime

may sometimes change a delinquent

into a solid citizen.

———✷———

PHILIP WYLIE

The education of children for God
is the most important
business done on earth.

R. L. BUBUEY

*T*hose who know, do.

Those who understand, teach.

———— ✳ ————

ARISTOTLE

The mediocre teacher tells.

The good teacher explains.

The superior teacher demonstrates.

The great teacher inspires.

———— ✳ ————

WILLIAM A. WARD

The art of teaching

is the art of assisting discovery.

———— ✳ ————

MARK VAN DOREN

A teacher who can arouse
a feeling for one single action,
for one single good poem,
accomplishes more than he
who fills our memory with rows
on rows of natural objects,
classified with name and form.

WOLFGANG VAN GOETHE

*T*eaching is a matter

of getting little fires started.

———✳———

THOMAS CARLYLE

Teaching at its best
is a kind of communion,
a meeting and merging of minds.

———✳———

EDGAR DALE

Delightful task!

To rear the tender thought,

To teach the young idea how to shoot.

———— ✳ ————

JAMES THOMSON

No one should teach who is not a bit awed

by the importance of the profession.

GEORGE FRASIER

*B*illions of fires can be set

by the light of a single candle,

and its light is multiplied.

A billion people can be enlightened

through one teacher,

and his teaching will increase.

——— ✳ ———

GEORGE M. LAMSA

A Teacher's Example

Always set a good example for others.
Be sincere and serious when you teach.

*
TITUS 2:7 CEV

*E*xample is the school of mankind,

and they will learn at no other.

———— ✳ ————

EDMUND BURKE

The greatest power for good

is the power of example.

*S*etting an example

is not the main means

of influencing others;

it is the only means.

ALBERT EINSTEIN

Children have never been good
at listening to their elders,
but they have never failed
to imitate them.

JAMES BALDWIN

A teacher affects eternity;

he can never tell

where his influence stops.

———✳———

HENRY BROOKS ADAMS

A Teacher's Patience

Let us not grow weary while doing good,

for in due season we shall reap

if we do not lose heart.

—❋—

GALATIANS 6:9 NKJV

I think it's important to teach

our children—as the Bible says—

line upon line, precept upon precept,

here a little, there a little.

If you try to teach a child

too rapidly, much will be lost.

RUTH GRAHAM

I touch the future. I teach.

CHRISTA MCAULIFFE

If you plan for a decade,

plant trees.

If you plan for a century,

teach the children.

People seldom see
the halting and painful steps
at which the most
insignificant success is achieved.

ANNE SULLIVAN

A courage which looks easy and yet is rare;

the courage of a teacher repeating,

day after day, the same lessons—

the least rewarded of all forms of courage.

———✳———

DE BALZAC

*Appreciation is that happy day
in the life of a teacher when a student says,
"I enjoyed being in your class today."*

PAUL McCLURE

To reach a child's mind,

a teacher must capture his heart.

Only if a child feels right

can he think right.

———— ✳ ————

HAIM G. GINOTT

A Teacher's Insight

Have two goals: wisdom—that is, knowing

and doing right—and common sense.

Don't let them slip away, for they fill you

with living energy, and are a feather in your cap.

———— ✳ ————

PROVERBS 3:21, 22 TLB

Teaching children to count

is not as important

as teaching them what counts.

The work will wait
while you show the child the rainbow,
but the rainbow won't wait
while you do the work.

———✳———

PATRICIA CLAFFORD

*T*oo often we give our children

answers to remember

rather than problems to solve.

——— ✳ ———

ROGER LEWIN

All the flowers of all the tomorrows
are in the seeds of today.

CHINESE PROVERB

True education doesn't merely

bring us learning, but love of learning;

not merely work but love of work.

Education is not the filling of a pail,
but the lighting of a fire.

WILLIAM BUTLER YEATS

*G*ood teaching

is one-fourth preparation

and three-fourths theater.

———— ✳ ————

GAIL GODWIN

It's not what is poured

into a student that counts,

but what is planted.

If in instructing a child,

you are vexed with it

for want of adroitness, try,

if you have never tried before,

to write with your left hand,

and then remember

that a child is all left hand.

J. F. BOYLE

To stimulate life, leaving it then free
to develop, to unfold, herein lies
the first task of the teacher.

———✳———

MARIA MONTESSORI

Don't judge each day

by the harvest you reap,

but by the seeds you plant.

ROBERT LOUIS STEVENSON

Who is not able to recall

the impact of some particular teacher—

an enthusiast, a devotee of a point of view,

a disciplinarian whose ardor came from

love of a subject, a playful but serious mind?

There are many images, and they are precious.

———— ✳ ————

JEROME BRUNER

People who teach us, bless us,

encourage us, support us, uplift us

in the dailyness of life.

We never tell them.

I don't know why, but we don't.

———✳———

ROBERT FULGHUM

In Praise of Teachers

We must always thank God for you.
And we should do this because it is right.

— ✳ —

2 THESSALONIANS 1:3 NCV

My mom is my favorite teacher.

She home schools me. She helps me

find out how butterflies move their wings.

———✳———

BRENNA, AGE 7

For almost 40 years, my third grade
teacher has continued to inspire me.
Through annual Christmas cards,
Mrs. Sauer has continued teaching me
about the things that matter most—
lovingly caring for her disabled daughter,
playing in a jazz band well into her 70s,
and nurturing lifelong friends.

VICKI, AGE 47

My favorite teacher is Miss Thompson.

She has plenty of bandaids in case

someone is bleeding on the playground.

MIKALA, AGE 6

Mr. McConnell was my English teacher.
He had a great sense of humor,
but was no nonsense when it came to
teaching grammar, punctuation,
creative writing, and more. He proved
that students could learn in a fun,
but structured environment.
His class was one that I always
looked forward to attending, and now,
all these years later, I can see and appreciate
the influence that he had on my life.

MARTHA, AGE 52

My favorite teacher is Miss Swenson.

She makes funny faces in the lunch line

and gives us second chances

when we forget to do our homework.

JONATHAN, AGE 9

*Mrs. Keane was my eighth grade
English teacher. Her writing exercises
lifted my imagination to the high sierra
of creativity. She inspired me to believe
in my writing—tortured characters and all.
I owe my first novel to her selfless giving,
a kindness never forgotten.*

SHELLEY, AGE 39

Mr. Sullivan said I had an excellent mind.

Somehow that one solitary affirmation

introduced me to a whole new world of possibility.

I never looked back. From then on,

I was convinced I could be anything I wanted to be.

———— ✳ ————

TIM, AGE 25

Even behind her black-rimmed glasses,
Mrs. Woods' sparkling blue eyes
reflected her enthusiasm for teaching
the art of penmanship. She not only taught
the importance of neatness and flow
of writing, but how writing mirrored
our individual "signature" in life.
Occasionally, I still find myself doodling
Mrs. Woods' penmanship exercises.

SUSAN, AGE 52

I like my teacher, Miss Smiley.

She dances around when we sing

the "Let's Get Started" song.

———✳———

ETHAN, AGE 5

"What color are you today?"
This is only one of Mrs. MacGilvra's
famous 9th Grade English roll call questions.
She taught us much more than grammar.
I learned how to let my imagination out
onto paper and how to dream big!
I always knew, from day one, that she
believed in me and what I could do.
It made all the difference.

WENDY, AGE 38

Mr. Smith, a short, bug-eyed English teacher had a passion for words. Something in my writing caught his attention and Mr. Smith encouraged me to work on the school newspaper. It was there that I took my first steps toward a publishing career. I'll always be grateful to him.

———— ✳ ————

TERRY, AGE 50

Mrs. Floyd was my junior high speech

and drama teacher. To this day,

I wonder what her secret formula was

for turning a bunch of shy,

awkward students into confident actors

and actresses who could impress

even the toughest theater critic!

———— ✳ ————

CHERIE, AGE 23